VANISHING HITCHHIKER

This series features unsolved mysteries, urban legends, and other curious stories. Each creepy, shocking, or befuddling book focuses on what people believe and hear. True or not? That's for you to decide!

45th Parallel Press

Published in the United States of America by Cherry Lake Publishing
Ann Arbor, Michigan
www.cherrylakepublishing.com

Author: Virginia Loh-Hagan
Reading Adviser: Marla Conn MS, Ed., Literacy specialist, Read-Ability, Inc.
Book Designer: Felicia Macheske

Photo Credits: © Joe Prachatree/Shutterstock.com, cover; © VERSUSstudio/Shutterstock.com, 5; © kenny1/Shutterstock.com, 7; © Maya Kruchankova/Shutterstock.com, 8; © Rawpixel.com/Shutterstock.com, 11; Kwangmoozaa/Shutterstock.com, 13;© nata-lunata/Shutterstock.com, 14; © Orhan Cam/Shutterstock.com, 17; © Delpixel/Shutterstock.com, 18; © maradon 333/Shutterstock.com, 21; © Ricardo Reitmeyer/Shutterstock.com, 22; © anyaivanova/Shutterstock.com, 25; © javarman/Shutterstock.com, 26; © Kamira/Shutterstock.com, 29

Graphic Elements Throughout: © iofoto/Shutterstock.com; © COLCU/Shutterstock.com; © spacedrone808/Shutterstock.com; © rf.vector.stock/Shutterstock.com; © donatas1205/Shutterstock.com; © cluckva/Shutterstock.com; © Eky Studio/Shutterstock.com

Copyright © 2018 by Cherry Lake Publishing
All rights reserved. No part of this book may be reproduced or utilized in any form or by any means without written permission from the publisher.

45th Parallel Press is an imprint of Cherry Lake Publishing.

Library of Congress Cataloging-in-Publication Data

Names: Loh-Hagan, Virginia, author.
Title: Vanishing hitchhiker / by Dr. Virginia Loh-Hagan.
Description: Ann Arbor : Cherry Lake Publishing, 2018. | Series: Urban legends: don't read alone! | Includes bibliographical references and index.
Identifiers: LCCN 2017035950| ISBN 9781534107649 (hardcover) | ISBN 9781534109629 (pdf) | ISBN 9781534108639 (pbk.) | ISBN 9781534120617 (hosted ebook)
Subjects: LCSH: Ghosts—Juvenile literature. | Hitchhiking—Miscellanea—Juvenile literature.
Classification: LCC BF1461 .L596 2018 | DDC 133.1/4—dc23
LC record available at https://lccn.loc.gov/2017035950

Cherry Lake Publishing would like to acknowledge the work of The Partnership for 21st Century Skills.
Please visit *www.p21.org* for more information.

Printed in the United States of America
Corporate Graphics

TABLE OF CONTENTS

Chapter One
INTO THIN AIR 4

Chapter Two
GHOSTLY STORIES 10

Chapter Three
GHOSTS OF THE ROADS 16

Chapter Four
SEEKING GHOSTLY ANSWERS 20

Chapter Five
TO HITCHHIKE OR NOT TO HITCHHIKE? 24

DID YOU KNOW? 30
CONSIDER THIS! 31
LEARN MORE 31
GLOSSARY 32
INDEX 32
ABOUT THE AUTHOR 32

Chapter One

INTO THIN AIR

What is a hitchhiker? Who was the vanishing hitchhiker?

Rob Davies and Chris Felton were driving. They saw a **hitchhiker**. Hitchhikers are people. They travel by getting free rides. They wait at the side of road. They wave down drivers.

Davies and Felton didn't stop driving. But they filmed the hitchhiker as they drove past. They went back. The hitchhiker had **vanished**. Vanish means to disappear. Had they seen a ghost?

The hitchhiker had been wearing an old military uniform. A military plane had crashed near that road. The crash happened in the 1940s. John Knight was the pilot. He died in that crash. People think he's a ghost. They think he's the vanishing hitchhiker.

Hitchhikers usually stick their thumbs out to get rides.

CONSIDER THE
EVIDENCE

Many countries have their own vanishing hitchhiker stories. There's a story in Senegal, Africa. A young taxi driver goes to a dance. He meets a woman. He walks her home. He gives her his sweater. He goes to her home the next day. He finds an old woman. The old woman said her daughter died. They go to her grave. They find his sweater on the tombstone. There's a story in Switzerland. An old woman is seen at Belchen Tunnel. Drivers slow down when they see her. The woman hitches a ride. She looks sick. Drivers ask how she is. The woman tells them something bad will happen. Then, she vanishes.

There's another story about a vanishing hitchhiker. It's about a woman named **Resurrection** Mary. Resurrection means to bring back to life after death. Jerry Palus met Mary in 1939. He met her at a dance. He drove her home. Mary wanted to stop at Resurrection **Cemetery**. Cemeteries are places where dead bodies are buried. Mary got out of the car. She walked to the cemetery. She vanished. Palus went to Mary's house. Mary's mother said Mary had died 5 years ago.

Mary was seen hitchhiking after that. She was sighted several times. In 1979, a cab driver stopped. He was at the cemetery. He picked up Mary. Then, she vanished.

Resurrection Cemetery is in Chicago.

People say they see Mary in a fancy white party dress.

In 1980, Clare Rudnicki saw her. She drove by the cemetery. She saw a girl walking. She saw bright light. She drove past. She turned around. The ghost vanished.

In 1989, Janet Kalal drove to the cemetery. She saw a woman in white. The woman stepped in front of her car. Kalal hit her. Then, the ghost vanished.

People think Resurrection Mary is Mary Bregovy's ghost. Bregovy went to a dance with her boyfriend. They got into a fight. Bregovy left. She walked. A car hit her. The driver ran away. This happened in 1934. Bregovy was buried in Resurrection Cemetery. She was buried in a white gown.

Chapter Two

GHOSTLY STORIES

What are the main features of the vanishing hitchhiker story? What are other versions of the story?

The vanishing hitchhiker is a popular **urban legend**. Urban means city. Legend means story. Urban legends are stories that were created in modern times. They're created by people who live in cities. They don't have to take place in cities.

The vanishing hitchhiker has other names. There's the ghostly hitchhiker. There's the **phantom** hitchhiker.

Phantom means ghost. Jan Harold Brunvand studies folktales. He said this story is "the most often collected and the most discussed **contemporary** legend of all." Contemporary means modern.

Urban legends are passed down from person to person.

SPOTLIGHT BIOGRAPHY

Ana Bakran is a hitchhiker. She was named "Adventurer of the Year." She hitchhiked from Zagreb to Bora Bora. Zagreb is in Croatia. Bora Bora is in the South Pacific. These places are over 10,000 miles (16,093 kilometers) apart. Bakran finished this trip in 2016. She did it in 3 years and 8 months. She traveled through 25 countries. She hitched rides in cars, trucks, motorcycles, boats, and helicopters, and even on horses. She slept anywhere she could. She blogged about her adventures. She said, "My first year of travelling, I travelled with 18 different hitchhikers. The rest of my journey, I hitchhiked alone."

The story starts with someone driving a car. The driver meets a hitchhiker. The hitchhiker is usually alone. The hitchhiker vanishes.

The hitchhiker is usually a young woman. The woman sees a car. She asks for a ride. She vanishes. She leaves something behind. The driver goes to return the item. The driver meets a relative of the woman. The relative tells the driver that the woman has been dead for years.

The hitchhiker turns out to be a ghost. The ghost is of a woman who died. The most common cause of death is a car crash. The ghost returns on special days.

Ghosts usually return on the anniversaries of their deaths.

New Zealand's urban legend includes a woman and her kitten.

There are many versions of the vanishing hitchhiker story. They're told all over the world.

In Germany, there's a hitchhiking nun ghost. Drivers pick her up. The nun only speaks in Latin. Then, she vanishes.

Italy also has nun ghost stories. Only Catholic drivers can see the nun. The nun tells them they're going to die.

There's a New Zealand story. A woman holds a kitten. She appears to be hitchhiking. Drivers pull over. Then, the woman and kitten vanish.

Chapter Three

GHOSTS OF THE ROAD

What are some of the earliest stories about the vanishing hitchhiker? How long have these stories been around?

The vanishing hitchhiker story has been around for many years. The Bible has a version. It's in the New Testament. An Ethiopian drives a **chariot**. Chariots are carts pulled by horses. The driver picks up Peter. Peter is a saint. Peter makes him a Christian. Then, Peter vanishes. In the United States, one story started in the 1870s. Early stories had a **stagecoach**. Stagecoaches are wagons pulled by horses.

One of the early stories is from the 1940s. Pearl Harbor in Hawaii just got attacked. A man gives a ride to a woman. The woman offers to pay for gas. The man says no. The woman tells him his future instead.

There are many stories about ghosts by the road.

The vanishing hitchhiker story became popular when cars were invented.

She said he would have a dead body in his car. She said Hitler would die in 6 months. Hitler was a German leader during World War II. Then, the woman vanished. The man drove home. He saw an accident. He took a man to the hospital. But the man died in his car. The first part of the woman's prediction came true. People wanted the second part to be true. They wanted Hitler to die. They wanted the war to end. The war did end and Hitler did die. But it wasn't until 5 years later.

In 1981, Brunvand wrote a book about the vanishing hitchhiker. This made the story popular. Over time, details of the story changed. But there's always a hitchhiker that vanishes.

REAL-WORLD CONNECTION

It was around July 4th. There was a couple. They were driving from Washington, D.C., to Boston. They stopped in northern Virginia. They went to a coffee shop. They saw a black kitten. They saw it run down a sidewalk. They left. The kitten hitchhiked. It slipped under their car. It crawled into their engine. The couple traveled 250 more miles (402 km). They heard meow sounds. They stopped in New York City. They opened the hood of their car. They found the kitten. They named it Coffee. He was 2 months old. Coffee was taken to an animal shelter.

Chapter Four

SEEKING GHOSTLY ANSWERS

What does the vanishing hitchhiker story mean? Why do parents tell this story?

Some experts think the story tells us about ourselves. The vanishing hitchhiker is not like other ghost stories. There's no violence. This ghost story is about a quick **encounter** between the living and the dead. Encounters are meetings. The ghosts are sad. They're stuck between life and death. They can't rest in peace. Drivers don't go looking for ghosts. The ghosts come to them. This means ghosts are everywhere. Drivers think the ghosts are humans at first. This means ghosts can be anyone. Drivers are regular people. This means ghost encounters can happen to anyone.

The drivers in the stories are good people. They're helpful.

People are confused about what happens after death. These stories are a warning. They remind people of **mortality**. Mortality is the cycle of life. Living things live, then die.

The stories are about **grief**. Grief is sad feelings. People feel sad when loved ones die. Relatives grieve for them. The ghosts grieve for their homes and family.

Some experts think parents like to tell this story. They want to warn their children. They don't want their children to hitchhike. Hitchhiking can be dangerous. Parents want children to stay away from dangerous strangers.

The story may be telling people to live life to the fullest.

INVESTIGATION TIPS

- Talk to someone who has seen a ghost while on the road. Ask them what they saw. Ask them how they felt. Get as many details as you can.

- Never go anywhere alone.

- Let people know where you are. Take pictures of your locations. Text them to a close friend. Do this often.

- Keep a cell phone with you at all times. Include emergency numbers. Bring a charger.

- Stay safe. Make good choices. Keep away from danger.

Chapter Five

TO HITCHHIKE OR NOT TO HITCHHIKE?

What are hallucinations? How did hitchhiking become unpopular?

Scientists think people who report seeing ghosts are **hallucinating**. People who see ghosts are mistaken. They see things that aren't there. Their eyes are playing tricks on them. Hallucinations are fake images.

But hitchhiking is real. Hitchhiking used to be a common practice. Many people would hitchhike across the country. Not many people owned cars. So, it made sense to hitch rides.

People liked meeting new people. Gillian Christie is a business owner. She hitchhiked in the 1970s. She hitchhiked from Colorado to Alaska. She did this during her college spring break.

Scientists don't believe in ghosts.

In many places, hitchhiking on the highway is against the law.

Hitchhiking meant freedom. It was part of the American dream. People liked to move around. They liked the idea of getting on the road. They liked going to different places.

Today, many people have their own cars. Also, people like having plans. They travel to specific places. Hitchhiking is not as popular. It also has a bad **reputation**. Reputation refers to what other people think. Today, many people think hitchhiking is dangerous. This is mainly because of urban legends. In some stories, drivers kill hitchhikers. In other stories, hitchhikers kill drivers. In the vanishing hitchhiker stories, drivers meet ghosts. Many people find this creepy. They stopped trusting drivers and hitchhikers.

EXPLAINED BY SCIENCE

Animals hitchhike all the time. An example is boa constrictors. Boas are snakes. They live in Aruba. They hitchhike. They take advantage of human movement. They crawl into parked cars. They hop off wherever the car ends up. They make babies. They take over areas. Another example is zebra mussels. Zebra mussels are from Russia. They hitchhiked on boats. They came to North America. Plants also hitchhike. They travel on people. They travel on the wind. One plant makes a lot of seeds. They drop seeds. They grow. This is how they take over areas. An example is Bathurst Burr. These plants are from Chile. They hitchhiked on horse tails.

Sadly, bad things have happened. In 1952, Connie Smith was 10 years old. She was at camp. She argued with another camper. She left. She hitchhiked home. She vanished.

In 1982, two women were killed while hitchhiking. They were killed at different times. But the killer left an orange sock at each crime scene. This happened in Colorado.

In 1988, Philip Fraser was on his way to college. He picked up a hitchhiker. He was killed. His body was found in a hole. The hitchhiker stole Fraser's car. He pretended to be Fraser. He was never caught.

These real stories have made the vanishing hitchhiker stories scarier. Real or not? It doesn't matter. The vanishing hitchhiker lives in people's imaginations.

Urban legends feed off people's real fears.

DID YOU KNOW?

- In 1998, Kmart ran an ad. It was selling Route 66 jeans. It featured the vanishing hitchhiker story.

- Blue Bell Hill is in England. It has a vanishing hitchhiker story. A young girl falls to the ground. She bleeds on a blanket. Drivers stop to help. She asks, "Why did you hit me?" Drivers get the cops. When cops come, the girl is gone. But the bloody blanket stays.

- There are many sightings of Resurrection Mary. People see Mary at dance clubs, in cabs, and walking by the cemetery. These witnesses can be trusted. They're trustworthy people. They don't claim to see any other ghosts.

- In some stories, the hitchhiker gives a warning about the future.

- In 1941, a TV show featured Lucille Fletcher's story "The Hitch-Hiker." In it, the driver was the ghost. The hitchhiker was alive.

- Richard Beardsley and Rosalie Hankey study folktales. They studied the vanishing hitchhiker stories. They did this in the 1940s. They collected more than 79 stories.

- Today's stories are about the "prom night" hitchhiker. It takes place on prom night. Prom is a special high school dance.

CONSIDER THIS!

Take a Position: Think about the pros and cons of hitchhiking. Do you think people should hitchhike? Why or why not? Argue your point with reasons and evidence.

Say What? Read the 45th Parallel Press book about Hookman. Compare Hookman and the vanishing hitchhiker. Explain how they're the same. Explain how they're different.

Think About It! Think about the different versions of the vanishing hitchhiker story. Write your own version.

LEARN MORE

- Apps, Roy, and Ollie Cuthbertson (illus.). Deadly Tales: *The Bloody Hook and Vanishing Hitchhiker*. Danbury, CT: Franklin Watts, 2012.
- Schwartz, Alvin, and Brett Helquist (illus.). *Scary Stories to Tell in the Dark*. New York: HarperCollins, 2007.

GLOSSARY

cemetery (SEM-ih-ter-ee) place where dead bodies are buried

chariot (CHAR-ee-uht) cart with two wheels pulled by horses

contemporary (kuhn-TEM-puh-rer-ee) modern

encounter (en-KOUN-tur) meeting

grief (GREEF) sadness felt after the death of a loved one

hallucinating (huh-LOO-suh-nay-ting) seeing things that aren't there

hitchhiker (HICH-hike-ur) person who waits by roads and gets free rides from strangers

mortality (mor-TAL-ih-tee) cycle of life, living things live and die

phantom (FAN-tuhm) ghost

reputation (rep-yoo-TAY-shuhn) what others think about someone or something

resurrection (rez-uh-REK-shuhn) returning from being dead

stagecoach (STAYJ-kohch) a wagon pulled by horses

urban legend (UR-buhn LEJ-uhnd) modern folktale that was popular at a time when more people lived in the cities

vanished (VAN-ishd) disappeared

INDEX

animals, 28
Bakran, Ana, 12
Bregovy, Mary, 9
Brunvand, Jan Harold, 11, 18
car crash, 13
death, 22
ghosts, 4–5, 9, 11, 13, 15, 17, 20–21, 24, 25, 30
grief, 22
hallucinations, 24
hitchhiking, 4, 12, 24–27, 29
kitten, hitchhiking, 19
Knight, John, 5
phantom, 10–11
plane crash, 5
Resurrection Mary, 7–9, 30
urban legends, 10–11, 27, 29
vanishing hitchhiker, 5
  early stories about, 16–18
  main features of stories about, 10, 13
  in other countries, 6, 15, 30
  other names for, 10
  versions of, 15, 30
  what the story means, 20–22

ABOUT THE AUTHOR

Dr. Virginia Loh-Hagan is an author, university professor, former classroom teacher, and curriculum designer. She used to hitch rides from Charlottesville to Blacksburg. She lives in San Diego with her very tall husband and very naughty dogs. To learn more about her, visit www.virginialoh.com.